——— The ———

Richard Streicher Jr.

MURDER

The

Richard Streicher Jr.

MURDER

Ypsilanti's Depot Town Mystery

GREGORY A. FOURNIER

Photos courtesy of the Ypsilanti Historical
Society

*The Richard Streicher Jr. Murder: Ypsilanti's
Depot Town Mystery*

Published by Wheatmark®
2030 East Speedway Boulevard, Suite 106
Tucson, Arizona 85719 USA
www.wheatmark.com

ISBN: 978-1-62787-612-4 (paperback)
ISBN: 978-1-62787-613-1 (ebook)
LCCN: 2018941607

Dedicated to the memory of seven-year-old Richard Streicher Jr., who died an ignominious death and was almost forgotten after eighty years of neglect.

Contents

Acknowledgments

The Richard Streicher Jr. Murder recounts the Depression-era murder that outraged local residents. The story was made possible by Ypsilanti Historical Society docents George Ridenour and Lyle McDermott. Between the years 2007 and 2011, George and Lyle used the Freedom of Information Act to gather official documents from the Michigan State Police; they scoured Michigan newspapers for vintage articles; and they conducted living history interviews with several of Richie's classmates—then in their eighties—who remembered him from school.

When George died after a long illness in 2015, Lyle asked me at the behest of the Ypsilanti Historical Society if I would take on the Streicher project. In George's name, I hope I did justice to his vision and to Richie's memory.

All photographs used in the making of this book are courtesy of the Ypsilanti Historical Society unless otherwise noted.

I also want to thank my beta readers, all of whom have deep roots in Ypsilanti: Melissa (Dusbiber) Hunt-Loy, Sally Foster, Janice Anschuetz, and Robert Anschuetz. Their insights, observations, and comments helped make the writing of this difficult-to-tell story a better experience for readers.

And last, a special thank you to Michelle Waters—forensic investigator and mortuary technician—for her help interpreting the autopsy reports.

—— The ——

Richard Streicher Jr.

MURDER

— 1 —

Establishing Time and Place

Ypsilanti, Michigan, was a ramshackle frontier town on the new Chicago Road in 1828 when pioneer Mark Norris and his family settled just east of the Huron River. Perhaps more than any other citizen, Norris advanced the development of the early city. He was an industrious, shrewd businessman. It was Norris who convinced the Michigan Central Railroad to make Ypsilanti a scheduled stop on their rail line and construct a loading dock and freight warehouse, giving birth to Depot Town.

The first train arrived on February 2, 1838. Overnight, Ypsilanti was no longer an isolated frontier town. It became the economic hub for the area's growing agricultural and manufacturing concerns. A thriving two-block-long commercial district grew up along both sides of East Cross Street. Depot Town businesses on the ground floor catered to the needs of weary travelers and local residents living on both sides of the Huron River. The upper floors were used for lodging, warehousing, or residential use. The Michigan Central Railroad built a three-story, red-brick train station crowned with a tall tower near the intersection of Cross and River streets. The Ypsilanti train station was said to be the finest between Detroit and Chicago. The second and third floors were for the stationmaster and his family. After a fire destroyed the upper floors in 1910, Michigan Central Railroad chose to rebuild only the ground floor.

Mark Norris built his water-powered flour mill on the northeast corner of Cross Street next to the Huron River sometime in the 1850s. The business changed hands several times over the years. The mill was damaged by fire in 1915 and rebuilt, but it became obsolete in the electrical age and was demolished in 1925. The old flour mill was gone, but the water raceway powering the waterwheel remained. In 1935 the Works Progress Administration (WPA) built a footbridge north of the Cross Street Bridge over the raceway leading to Frog Island Park, making it accessible from the Cross Street Bridge.

This public works project put a crew of local men to work during the height of the Great Depression when jobs were scarce and times were lean in Ypsilanti. Train stations throughout the land became magnets for displaced and shiftless people. Ypsilanti's train station was no different. Every mother warned her children to avoid Depot Town after dark—but times were tough. In the winter months, local kids would lay in wait for the trains to stop for five minutes, switch tracks, and pull out again. They would throw snowballs at the train in hopes that the coal tenders would retaliate and throw lumps of coal back at them. It was a game they played. Afterward, the kids gathered the coal and took it home for their coal stoves. Against this background, the body of a seven-year-old boy was found frozen to death beneath the Frog Island footbridge on March 8, 1935.

2

Lost and Then Found

On March 7, 1935, Richard (Richie) Streicher Jr. did not appear for dinner at six o'clock—the customary time for the Streicher family meal. Lucia Streicher searched the neighborhood on foot while Richard Streicher Sr. searched town in a borrowed car. When Richie didn't return home by 7:20 p.m., his father drove to the Ypsilanti police department to report his son missing. All available police were dispatched for the remainder of the evening to look for tracks in the fresh snow near the Streicher apartment located at 404 North Huron Street. The police also looked along the nearby Huron River bank, 250 feet east of the Streichers' doorstep. The general search was called off at midnight.

The next morning, Ypsilanti police chief Ralph Southard and Washtenaw County deputy sheriff Richard Klavitter went to the Streicher home to question the Streichers about what they thought might have happened to their son. Lucia did most of the talking while her husband, Richard, sat mute unless addressed directly.

In her initial statement to the police, Lucia became concerned when her husband asked why their son was not home for dinner. Lucia said she last saw Richie at four thirty when she was visiting Mrs. Eugene Dillon—the wife of the apartment house caretaker where the Streichers rented a back apartment. She told police that Mrs. Dillon disliked children. Richie was covered with wet snow when he brought in the evening newspaper, so she ushered him to their apartment. Lucia said she told Richie to go outside and play until suppertime.

The last time Lucia saw her son, he was headed across the street, pulling his sled to the Four Hills—a local expression for the terraced bluff behind the Daniel Quirk mansion on 300 North Huron Street overlooking the Huron River, the Cross Street Bridge, and Depot Town. From spring through autumn, a beautiful garden adorned the terraces, but during the winter, local youth commandeered the sloping terrain for sledding and tobogganing.

When Richie failed to return home for dinner, Lucia called his name from the sidewalk outside their apartment. That usually worked, but not this time. Lucia told Southard and Klavitter she put her coat on and walked down West Cross Street toward the river, calling Richie's name. When her son was nowhere to be found, Lucia turned around and walked up West Cross Street to Ypsilanti High School, one block from their apartment. The Ypsilanti Braves were hosting a basketball game. Thinking her son might be drawn to the game, Lucia had his name announced over the public-address system but again with no result.

Lucia returned home while her husband went to the family tool and die shop on River Street to borrow his sister's car. He searched the nearby streets and drove to the homes of Richie's classmates to see if Richie might be visiting one of them. His friends hadn't seen Richie since he left school. Richard Streicher Sr. returned home at seven thirty to see if his son had wandered home—he hadn't. Streicher drove to the Ypsilanti City Police at 56 North Huron Street to report his son missing. Next, he drove to the Michigan State Police post on Michigan Avenue to do the same. Streicher told the police he and his wife searched for their son while there was still daylight.

After he returned his sister's car, Richard said he continued searching with Ypsilanti Patrolman Joseph Sackman in his squad car. They looked for Richie's footprints behind the Neuhauser Chicken Hatchery and along the west bank of the Huron River; then they checked the nearby Streicher family tool and die shop grounds, including an outbuilding. The freshly fallen snow was undisturbed— no footprints were found.

Streicher asked Sackman if he would like to stop by the apartment for some hot coffee to warm up before continuing the search. Finally, they set out again, this time with Lucia, they searched until four o'clock in the morning when Sackman took them home.

Chief Southard and Deputy Sheriff Klavitter asked Lucia if their son may have run away. She and her husband didn't think so; then the Streichers were asked if they knew of anyone who might want to do harm to their son. Neither parent could think of anyone. In Klavitter's official report, he mentioned that Lucia sat in an easy chair manicuring her fingernails proclaiming if her son was not found by noon, she was confident her parents would receive a ransom letter because they were wealthy.

"My parents were very fond of Richie," Lucia said. Klavitter found it curious Lucia said "were" rather than "are" and mentioned it in his report.

Lucia implicated her brother-in-law, John Testo, in the hypothetical kidnapping. She believed revenge might be the motive because her parents gave her and Richard some money, but her parents refused to loan her sister, Erma, and her Italian husband, John Testo, five hundred dollars to open a beer garden in Elkhart, Indiana. Lucia told police Erma was "disowned" by their parents because she and her husband "lived by their wits and the rackets between Elkhart and Chicago." Lucia gave Klavitter John Testo's address. That was the first lead in the case.

Deputy Sheriff Klavitter noted in his report that during his inquiry Lucia laughed and joked with him while continuing to file her nails. "Mrs. Streicher was as much interested in exhibiting her legs as anything else," he wrote. "She wasn't at all disturbed about the disappearance of her son, it seemed to me."

Patrolman Sackman noted in his report of the previous evening's search that when he stepped inside the Streicher apartment for a cup of coffee, he saw Lucia casually knitting in an armchair with a ball of yarn on her lap. Sackman asked if she wanted to join the search. She reluctantly joined in. Sackman wrote that Mrs. Streicher said no fewer than five times, "I can't think but that Richie is in the river."

Sackman also noted that when they drove to the northeast end of the Cross Street Bridge, he stopped the squad car at the walkway leading to the Frog Island Bridge. When he started getting out of the car to look for footprints, both Streichers insisted they had "already searched all around there. Let's not waste time." Not wanting to contradict them, Sackman drove on.

Leaving the bridge, they searched the outskirts of town from the Peninsular Paper Company to the north and Ford Lake to the south. At about four o'clock that morning, the Streichers ran out of ideas where to look and were exhausted. Sackman drove them home. The patrolman documented that at no time while he and Mr. Streicher went searching did Mrs. Streicher venture out of the car.

———————

At noon the next day, thirteen-year-old Buck Holt and his eleven-year-old brother, Billy, followed muskrat tracks in the freshly fallen snow when they walked near the concrete footbridge leading to Frog Island Park. The brothers saw a child's body under the abutment connecting the footbridge to the Cross Street Bridge. Buck and Billy ran up the riverbank to Anderson's Service Station, where the old flour mill had been. The boys told twenty-two-year-old gas station attendant Raymond Deck that they found a dead kid under the footbridge. Deck left the gas station to take a quick look. When he returned, Deck phoned the Ypsilanti Police. Although still not formally identified, Richard Streicher Jr.'s body was found only four hundred feet from his apartment.

By the time the police arrived, a growing crowd of bystanders trampled any footprint evidence left in the overnight snow. The Ypsilanti police found the general disposition of the boy's body relaxed as if placed there with great care. It was frozen solid, the boy's arms positioned slightly outward from his torso. The body was pried from the frozen ground and taken to the Moore Funeral Home on 101 South Washington Street. Washtenaw County Coroner Dr. David N. Robb ordered a postmortem examination for later that evening.

Deputy Sheriff Klavitter and Chief Southard returned to the Streicher apartment to give the Streichers the news no parents want to hear. Lucia's brother, Ted Mueller, was in the apartment to show his sister moral support at the news that Richie was missing. When Lucia heard her son's body was found, she fell apart, Ted later told the press. "A doctor was called in to administer a shot to calm her down."

— 3 —

Coroner's Findings and Police Theories

An autopsy was performed by Dr. Stacey C. Howard at nine o'clock that evening at the Moore Funeral Home rather than the county morgue in Ann Arbor. In his report, Dr. Howard described the body as "a well-developed and well-nourished white male, age seven, height three foot six, weight sixty-eight pounds." Dr. Howard noted the boy's clothing was removed before the examination at the mother's behest, and the body was thoroughly cleansed by funeral parlor staff. This was highly irregular for a homicide case. It was quickly determined the boy's lungs were clear of water, indicating he had not drowned, and no foreign matter was found in the boy's oral cavity, indicating he hadn't choked to death.

Fourteen stab wounds were found on Richie's body. Eight shallow punctures on the left upper portion of his head penetrated the winter cap Richie was wearing but not his cranium. Two superficial slash wounds were found across the throat, but neither was the cause of death. These wounds did indicate to Dr. Howard that the murderer was right-handed. On the anterior surface of the boy's left chest, two superficial scratches roughly formed the letter Y over Richie's ribcage. Of the four stab wounds to the chest, three entered the heart, where the points on the Y met—any of which was fatal. Only one of the wounds nicked a rib; the others penetrated the third-interspace of the ribcage with direct entry into the heart. Dr. Howard estimated Richie's body lost three pints of blood, but no blood pool was found under or near the body. It was a certainty Richie Streicher was not killed where his body was found. Dr. Howard noted that all the chest wounds had "clean-cut edges as though made by a slender, sharp cutting instrument, like a double-edged stiletto."

The original police theory surmised the young boy was the victim of a hit-and-run accident on the Cross Street Bridge—his body quickly stashed under the footbridge to delay discovery so the driver could escape unnoticed. Once the autopsy was completed, the case clearly became a homicide. Police investigators quickly devised two new theories.

The first theory held that only a "depraved moron" could be capable of such an attack. "Degenerates, fiends, perverts, and sex maniacs" were labels used by police and *Ypsilanti Daily Press* reporters to refer to the men the police rounded up—despite there being no evidence the victim was sexually molested. It was routine policy to round up all the usual suspects. Any men in the area with a sex offense on their records, a child molestation charge, and known homosexuals were required to account for themselves on the afternoon Richie went missing. Individuals without solid alibis were jailed and held until their stories checked out. Much to the investigators' chagrin, every one of these men had alibis. Untold hours were wasted by investigators interrogating men innocent of committing a crime where no sexual offense or motive had been established.

The second theory held that a transient train passenger hopped off the train for a layover, and while in town, murdered an innocent seven-year-old boy who was unknown to him, then hopped back on the train without arousing suspicion or leaving a clue. The motive for this theory was likewise flimsy.

The third theory held that the nature of the wounds indicated this crime was committed by an enraged person rather than a full-blown maniac. Bloodlust was ruled out as a motive. There was no frenzy of slash or hack marks on the body. When the boy died, the attack ended. The careful placement of his body under the footbridge led some investigators to believe a person close to him was more likely the murderer—someone who knew him—a friend or a relative. Perhaps more than one person was involved.

———

Several days later, Deputy Sheriff Klavitter returned to the Streicher apartment and carefully questioned the grieving mother. He asked Lucia if she had searched along the riverbank the previous night looking for her son.

She hesitated. "No. I wasn't around there, was I, Richard?"

"I don't believe so, Lou."

"Gas station attendant Raymond Deck reported he saw a woman's heel print in the fresh snow near where your son was found. What shoes were you wearing while searching for Richie?"

"Are you suggesting I killed my son?"

"I only want to follow up on what Deck saw. The Holt kid who found the body said he saw some woman's heel marks in the fresh snow too. Are you certain you didn't search along the millrace behind Anderson's garage Thursday evening?"

"If you think I was along the riverbank, you are mistaken."

Lucia marched into her bedroom and returned with three pairs of shoes. "I wore all of them searching for Richie last night and ruined them all. Do these look like the shoes?"

"I don't know. I wasn't able to get any measurements. The heel print was destroyed by a crowd of gawkers."

"Are you accusing me of killing my son?"

Klavitter backed off. In his report to Prosecutor Rapp, he said of his several interviews with Lucia Streicher, "She was always nervous when first approached, but as the interviews progressed, she gained fortitude and fight. The longer we talked, the tougher she got. From that day until now, Lucia has had it out for me. She threatened 'to bump me off' if the opportunity presented itself."

It was Deputy Sheriff Klavitter's theory that Richard Streicher Jr. was killed on the west side of the Huron River, taken under the Cross Street Bridge to the east bank, and placed under the footbridge. He reasoned that Richie was last seen sledding on the west side of the Huron River. The Streichers' apartment faced West Cross Street—the second busiest thoroughfare in town. Foot and automobile traffic to and from Depot Town across the bridge would have been heavy between four thirty and six o'clock—the window of opportunity when Richie disappeared. Not to mention it was still light outside. Moving a lifeless body over the bridge without notice was unlikely. Because Richie's clothing was soaked and frozen by the time the Holt brothers found the body the next afternoon, Richard's body must have come into contact with the river. The fact that no blood pool was found under the body or anywhere nearby strongly suggests the body and clothing may have been rinsed by the river current, leaving no apparent blood evidence. Whoever murdered the boy was yet to be determined, but Klavitter already had his suspicions. All he lacked was evidence.

As soon as the Streicher murder broke in the press, Ray Harrington, correspondent for the *Detroit Times,* rushed to interview Richie's maternal grandparents at their Scott Lake estate. Theodore Mueller was a design engineer and inventor for the Cadillac Motor Car Company. Police characterized him as "a Prussian German immigrant known to be an autocrat who ran his household with an iron fist." His wife, Maria Repphun, was said to be a "Romany Gypsie (sic), superstitious like her race, and obedient to her husband."

Harrington wrote in his article that a housekeeper admitted him to the Mueller house. He found Mrs. Mueller quietly reading a letter. When she looked up and asked Harrington what he wanted, he informed her that her grandson was found murdered. Mrs. Mueller cried out, "At last, she's done it. At last, she's done it."

Before Harrington could ask Mrs. Mueller whom she referred to, Mr. Mueller entered the room, ordering his wife to shut her mouth. He snatched the letter from her and ordered Harrington out of the house in no uncertain terms.

"My property is surrounded by a stone wall. The next time you step foot on it, I'll set my German shepherd guard dogs on you. We live very secluded lives, rarely entertain or go anywhere. We don't welcome intrusion of any sort." With that, Harrington beat a hasty retreat to file his story.

---— 4 ——

News Spreads and Gossip Grows

The *Ypsilanti Daily Press* (*YDP*) ran an article about Richie Streicher on March 9, 1935. Richie was a second grader at the special education Fresh Air School housed in Welch Hall on the campus of Michigan State Normal College—now Eastern Michigan University. The program was said to be for "children of low vitality." Students in the program had to have some sort of medical condition. Principal Paul J. Misner of Roosevelt School recalled having lunch with Richard on Tuesday before his death and was impressed by the young man's "evident alertness." Oran Denton, a janitor at the school, was quoted as saying, "The Streicher boy was a pleasant and intelligent sort of boy." Richie's teacher, Miss Elsie Munsolf, expressed her sorrow "at the loss of such a likeable boy." She said, "Richard was a fine-looking child, rosy cheeked and clear skinned. One of his happiest days was his seventh birthday, when his mother brought refreshments to school so all his classmates could enjoy the occasion with him. Everyone liked him. He was a charming fellow and always the center of our activities. He was very intelligent. I would give him an A grade in the three *R*s. Richard will be greatly missed by his classmates. He was always happy. His mother came by often to inquire about his progress. She always met him with a kiss and a smile, which she extended to all the pupils."

Paul Woodside attended classes with Richie Streicher and walked home with him the day he disappeared. He told the *YDP* reporter that Richie was smiling and happy the last time he saw him. Mrs. Woodside, Paul's mother, was quoted in the article as saying, "Richard was unusually bright and well-minded." Gas station attendant Raymond Deck, who phoned police with the discovery of Richie's body, remarked, "I used to call Richie 'Sauerkraut' to tease him because of his German accent. He was a good kid."

Police investigators discovered from Richard Streicher Sr. that his son attended kindergarten in Detroit in 1932. The family moved back to Ypsilanti and enrolled Richie in first grade at Saint John the Baptist Parochial School for the 1933–1934 school year. For second grade, the Streichers chose the special education Fresh Air School at the Normal College—no reason given. Investigators asked whether Richie's teacher at the Fresh Air School ever sent any bad reports home about his son's conduct. Streicher answered no. Then the state police investigator asked if Richie was hard to handle.

"My son was troublesome at times, but no more than the average boy. He was full of the devil with more pep than the average boy." Why Richie was enrolled in special education classes has never been firmly established. Eighty-year-old Paul Woodside was interviewed in 2007. Woodside thought Richie may have had a heart condition, but he wasn't sure.

Upon further examination, Depot Town merchants and neighbors had a somewhat different portrayal of Richie. They told police he was known to tease other children, annoy shopkeepers, and often didn't obey his parents, but none of the local business owners was willing to go on the record.

When news circulated around town that Richie was murdered, several people came forward to police with information. Mr. Walter Purdy lived at 416 North Huron Street, a few houses down from the Streicher apartment. At seven fifteen or seven thirty that evening, he and his wife heard a child scream twice—not a scream of glee but one of terror. Purdy thought the sound came from near the footbridge off Cross Street on the east side of the river. He went outside but was unable to hear or see anything. Purdy and his wife figured children were playing when someone fell into the river. The next day, he heard from neighbors that the Streicher boy was found murdered under the footbridge. Police considered Purdy's information a solid clue to set probable time of death.

In the early afternoon of the day Richie went missing, census taker Mrs. Eugene B. Staebler was in the Streicher apartment gathering routine census information. In the course of answering routine questions, Lucia Streicher stated she was separated from her husband and wondered if that made her head of household for income tax purposes. Then Lucia inquired about the procedure and expense of getting a divorce. The conversation seemed odd to the census taker, who had never met Lucia before.

Mrs. Staebler felt duty bound to write a letter to Ypsilanti Police Chief Southhard:

"As soon as I heard of the death of Richard Streicher Jr., I thought that his mother committed the crime...I took her census on that afternoon. I just can't forget how she looked. She said she had a headache. I was a total stranger, but she went on at length and told me of her trouble with her husband. How he had signed away his rights to his child. She was at her wits end to know how she was to handle her family affairs. It occurred to me she felt if she divorced her husband, she wouldn't be free as long as the child was hers. Someone who knows Lucia Streicher remarked to me that she had been very cross to her child...She told me that the father was not living at home, so she was no doubt alone with her son when he returned home. Mrs. Streicher was irritable with a headache and possibly struck her son. Maybe she hit him harder than she thought and had to finish the job to cover up her bad temper. Mrs. Streicher told me there was nothing could be done to bring about reconciliation with her husband. When I read (in the newspapers) of the endearing expressions she used when she went to see the child at the funeral home, it made me think she was a pretty good actor. I ask that these personal matters of the Streichers' home life be kept confidential. I am an enumerator of the census and under oath to keep information confidential. However, I feel that if this information could help in way of clearing up this mystery, I should tell you."

Chief Southard found Mrs. Staebler's letter compelling but long on opinion and short on fact. Still, the census taker had no apparent reason to lie.

A week before her son went missing, Lucia Streicher invited new neighbors—Mr. and Mrs. Tom Murray—to her apartment for chop suey dinner. In a statement made to the Ypsilanti Police a week after Richie's murder, the Murrays claimed Lucia told them she was pregnant with Clinton LeForge's baby. She added that LeForge was her lawyer. The Murrays were surprised she would reveal such an intimate detail of her private life to virtual strangers. Tom Murray told police that when Richie came home late for dinner, Lucia lost control and slapped her son hard in the face, telling him, "Don't cry damn you!"

The Murrays said that on the day the boy went missing, the Streichers had a violent argument when Richard Sr. came home from work, which contradicted the census enumerator's assertion that Mr. Streicher did not live in the home. Other people who lived in the house heard the Streichers arguing too, but when questioned by police, the Streichers denied the argument happened.

Several of the Streicher neighbors on North Huron Street—Mrs. DeNike, Mrs. Horn, and Mrs. Freeman—sent a handwritten letter to Washtenaw County Prosecutor Albert J. Rapp. The letter began by saying they did not like getting involved because Lucia was their neighbor and they liked her, but they felt duty bound to pass on the following information.

We know, but not seeing with our own eyes, Richie went into the house, and Clinton LeForge was there. Lucia told her son to go outside. After a while, Richie told a friend he was sledding with that he was hungry, so he went back into the apartment. Nobody ever saw Richie come out. Mr. Rapp, the fact that the boy's body was cleaned up before the autopsy and his clothes were burned up at Lucia's request is suspicious enough. But she had Clinton LeForge remove everything the child ever had from his bedroom the day after he was murdered. Most mothers want to keep the things their little ones had. Now Lucia says she is anxious to get out of Ypsi. Clinton LeForge used to come by their house real often. One day Richie said, "I don't see why that man has to come here so often."

Mrs. Mildred McLaughlin lived in the same neighborhood and knew the Streichers. She told police, "They (the Streichers) were very peculiar. Lou (Lucia) was funny in many ways, but she used to abuse her son badly at times. The boy was a little cuss himself. He was always picking fights and did not get along well with other children his own age." These rumors cast new light on the investigation.

Another Streicher family neighbor, Mrs. Martha Dolph, reported to police that she was walking across the Huron River Bridge toward Depot Town at nine forty-five the evening before Richie's body was found. Dolph said she came upon a woman and two men talking. She overheard one of the men say, "It's all off now." The other man drew his hat down and turned his face away from her when she passed. Dolph decided the man was Clinton LeForge. She recognized his voice because LeForge had worked as a bouncer at the Eclipse Dance Hall, which the Dolphs operated on Ecorse Road. When questioned if the woman was Lucia Streicher, she answered, "I know Lucia, and the woman wasn't her."

Ypsilanti resident Herbert E. Hayes came forward and reported he saw LeForge walking south in the 200 block of Huron Street on March 7 between 7:20 p.m. and 7:30 p.m. Hayes said they acknowledged each other when they passed. LeForge was wearing a black overcoat and a slouch hat.

One thing was certain. There was serious dysfunction in the Streicher household, and Clinton LeForge became a person of keen interest. LeForge was a fifty-year-old attorney known locally as a collector of Indian relics and legends. He lived with his wife on a farm in Superior Township just north of Ypsilanti, but his law practice was located at 8 South Huron Street, just four blocks from the Streicher residence in Ypsilanti. Police investigators discovered that Lucia Streicher hired LeForge to handle her divorce case before her son's death.

— 5 —

Suspicion Mounts

Corporal Frank Walker went to the Streicher residence to question Lucia about Clinton LeForge. "I had a rift with my husband over money matters in 1933 and hired LeForge to represent me, but that has been settled. Richard and I have lived happily until this tragedy struck our home." Anyone who knew anything about the Streichers knew that statement wasn't true.

Walker asked about LeForge removing Richie's toys from his room. Lucia answered that it was too painful to see them. When asked why Clinton LeForge was so interested in this case, she answered he was the family's legal advisor and friend. After LeForge left the apartment, Lucia claimed she asked her husband to look in a box for a knife that she suspected LeForge had planted there, but none was found.

When Walker told her that LeForge was talking around town pointing the finger at her, she abruptly changed her attitude and called LeForge a liar, stating she would face him anytime. When asked what LeForge's motive was, Lucia said, "Revenge. We were at a party together and I rejected his advances. Clinton might be trying to get back at me." Lucia became sullen and answered the rest of Walker's questions with a simple yes or no. Walker's report noted she complained of having dizzy spells and said she was taking fifty aspirin a day because of severe pains in her head.

"Everyone in Ypsilanti believes I killed my boy," she said. "One day I felt like jumping in front of a passing truck and ending it all." On the window sill in her apartment, the investigator noticed a book entitled *The Perfect Crime.*

The next day, Corporal Walker interviewed Richard Streicher, asking if Lucia asked him to look for a knife in a box. He answered, "No, my wife lied." Streicher also revealed that Lucia lied when she said she never slapped Richie. He witnessed his wife slapping Richie in the face with an open hand a number of times.

A week after the murder, Lucia Streicher consented to an interview with Dorothy Williams of the *Ypsilanti Daily Press* to show the Streichers' togetherness and counter malicious neighborhood gossip. Clutching her arms and shuddering, she told Williams, "I hope I never see snow again. Somehow I feel if it hadn't snowed, Richie would be with us today. He went out to play in the snow. That was all. I never saw him again after that. Later when this is all over, I hope we can go far away to a country where we will never see snow again and forget all this."

With sad eyes and desperate voice, Lucia Streicher continued as she ran her hands over the crisp taffeta of her white dress. "I am wearing white for mourning because Richie liked me in white...I buried him in white too. I'll wear white for Richie and sometimes gray. I had such a time finding white too. I couldn't find a dress here (in Ypsilanti) that I wanted, so I went to Ann Arbor. I had to find a hat too that wouldn't be too frivolous."

When reporter Williams asked Lucia about the potted hyacinth on her windowsill, a smile lightened her face. "The children in

Richie's school sent it to me. Isn't it beautiful? They send me notes every day...telling me how good he was in arithmetic and drawing. Richie was the sweetest child. Nobody could have been sweeter. He brought in the paper to me and said he was going out to play some more." Suddenly, her expression darkened. "How could my boy have dropped so completely from sight? Someone must have seen him. He couldn't just disappear like that...I can't believe this has happened to us. Sometimes it seems as though Richie is still with us. When school time is over, I catch myself looking for him. All we can do now is try to bring the slayer to justice and save other children; then we must go away and try to forget."

A staged photograph of the grieving parents accompanied the article—Lucia sitting in an armchair with her husband standing next to her and holding her hand.

On March 15, 1935, the same day Lucia's article hit the newsstands, Michigan State Police Captain Donald. S. Leonard and his partner, Sergeant Phillip Hutson, interviewed thirteen-year-old Gerald Young at his home with his mother present. The eighth grader was the last known person to see Richie Streicher alive. From four o'clock to four thirty, Gerald Young and Richie were sledding on Richie's sled behind city hall across the street from the Streicher apartment.

Young sold magazines door-to-door to help his family make ends meet. He told Richie he had to make a magazine delivery and left. Richie told Young he was cold and going home. As Richie dragged his sled toward West Cross Street, a man in a black overcoat with a brown hat called out to him.

"What did the man say?" Captain Leonard asked.

"'Come here, sonny.'"

"Was it his father?"

"No."

"Do you know Mr. Clinton LeForge?"

"No."

"Did you see the man's face?"

"Not enough to say what he looked like."

"Did Richard act like he knew the man?"

"Yes, I guess so."

"When they went across the street, did Richie take his sled with him?"

"Sure."

"What kind of sled was it?"

"A Flexible Flyer."

"Did you see them enter the Streicher apartment?"

"No, I needed to go. I took off in another direction."

"Did Richie ever tell you about his parents quarreling?"

"No."

"Did he ever tell you anything about his mother and father whipping him?"

"Nope."

"Did Richie ever talk about running away from home?"

"I didn't know him or his family really. He's just a kid I sledded with sometimes. We weren't good friends or anything."

"Let's focus on the man you saw. How old would you say he was?"

"From what I could tell, he was seventeen or eighteen maybe. I didn't get a good look at him. He didn't look like an old man."

"How old do you think I am?" Captain Leonard asked.

"In your thirties maybe."

"And the man with Richie would be quite a bit younger than me?"

"Yeah, I'd say so."

"Would you say a high-school-aged boy?"

"No, I don't think that young."

"It's important we establish the age of this man."

"Yes, I know."

"Are you sure you saw the man yourself and not telling us what you heard from someone else?"

"No, Richie and me were the only ones there."

Sergeant Hutson took over. "Was the man as tall as me, Gerald?" He stood up.

"No, I think he was taller."

"Was he as heavy as me?"

"No."

"Was he well-dressed?"

"Yes, I guess so, only his overcoat looked too big on him."

"Let me ask you about Richie's clothing. What was he wearing?"

"A snow suit, high-top boots, red mittens, and a padded cap with earflaps and a chin strap."

"Was the chin strap fastened?"

"Not that I remember."

"Were his clothes wet?"

"We rolled in the snow quite a bit trying to trip each other off the sled, but it wasn't a wet snow. It was cold that day, so the snow was dry."

The state policemen thanked Gerald Young for his information and his mother for letting them interview her son. They knew Gerald's information had limited value, but it did account for the time leading up to Richie's disappearance. It helped police establish a tighter timeline.

6

New Person of Interest

Captain Leonard summoned Clinton LeForge to the Ypsilanti State Police post two weeks to the day after the murder. A stenographer took notes of the questioning.

"Mr. LeForge, do you make this statement voluntarily?"

"Yes."

"Where were you in the later part of the afternoon on Thursday, March seventh?"

"In my office."

"How late did you stay there?"

"Well, I would say at least until six thirty."

"Were you there alone?"

"No. There were other people there that afternoon."

"Who were they?"

"Lewis Smith, the blacksmith on South Huron Street."

"I know Lew," Captain Leonard said. "When was he there?"

"I would say at five o'clock."

"For how long?"

"He left between five thirty and five forty-five."

"Who else?"

"Joe Hooper, Circuit Court Commissioner and Ann Arbor attorney. He came by to drop off some legal papers."

"How late did he stay?"

"Maybe until six o'clock, maybe a little before. Not long, though."

"Who else?"

"John Matthews, owner of the tin shop next door."

"That's three; anyone else?"

"Yes, Ralph Edwards—the handyman who helped me install my new coal stove. I have the date on the receipt."

"That won't be necessary, Mr. LeForge. When did Matthews leave?"

"Before Mr. Smith came in."

"What about Edwards?"

"Sometime around five fifteen or so, after the stove was set up."

"Everyone left by six o'clock? How long did you stay in your office?"

"Until six thirty. I had to gather some paperwork for a client and close the office."

"So you were alone for about thirty minutes?"

"Yes. Something like that."

"Where did you go after you left your office?"

"I went to Diroff's grocery store on Michigan Avenue to pick up empty milk bottles for my son's dairy business. We listened to *Lowell Thomas* and *Amos and Andy* on the radio; then I went to the Chamberlain Inn on East Michigan Avenue."

"How did you get there?"

"I drove my car."

"Anyone with you?"

"No."

"Who can vouch for you at Chamberlain's?"

"Mrs. Mary Wilkie—her father, Clark Glazier, co-owns the business. She runs the bar. Clark wasn't there that night, but his partner, Frank Minni, was."

"Anyone else?"

"Someone named Albertson—I don't know his first name."

"Was he alone?"

"No, he was with a lady."

"Is that everyone?"

"No! Ypsilanti policeman Ernie Rowe came in too. He was a friend of Albertson."

"What did you do when you got to Chamberlain's?"

"I took three copies of a bill of complaint and presented them to Minni."

"What was the nature of the complaint?"

"Back rent and eviction notice. I read the complaint to Frank Minni and Mary Wilkie, stressing how necessary it was to get it signed or risk default, and then I ordered supper and ate with Albertson and his friend."

"How long did you stay there?"

"Until eleven thirty—maybe later."

"Then where did you go?"

"Back to my office to fire up my stove. I had trouble starting the coal because it was all new to me. I was used to my old wood-burning stove. Afterward, I stopped by the Ypsi police station to see my friend Officer Bill Morey before he started his shift."

"What time?"

"Around midnight."

"Did you see Morey?"

"No, I was in the toilet when Bill came on duty. I missed him."

"Then what?"

"I went home."

"When did you arrive home?"

"Around one o'clock."

"While you were at the police station, did any of the officers mention the disappearance of Richie Streicher?"

"No, I found out the next day when Mrs. Baker told my wife in my office."

"What did Mrs. Baker tell you?"

"She said, 'Did you hear? Little Richard Streicher has disappeared.' I think that was the way she put it."

"Did you know Richie Streicher?"

"Yes, I've seen him a few times."

"Did you see him on the day he disappeared?"

"No, I was busy in my office."

"On the day after Richie's body was found, you removed all of his toys from his bedroom, did you not?"

"Yes, I did."

"At whose request?"

"The grieving mother, Mrs. Streicher."

"Lucia, also known as Lucy?"

"Yes."

"Was this in your capacity as a lawyer or friend?"

"Both."

"Why did she ask you and not her husband to take the boy's toys away?"

"They were barely on speaking terms."

"Have you ever handled legal matters for Lucia Streicher?"

"Yes. I filed a divorce proceeding for her, but she dropped the case."

"For what reason?"

"The Streichers reconciled."

"Mr. LeForge, were you romantically involved with Lucia at the time?"

"No!"

"How about now?"

"Never! That woman is hell. I once saw Lucia strike her husband hard on the Adam's apple sticking his windpipe together. Lucia is as strong as a man. He had a close call. I couldn't live with that woman for five minutes. I don't know how Dick stands it."

"When was the last time you saw Richie Streicher?"

"In 1933 he was in my office with his mother, bothering a helper of mine named Chris."

"One last question. Who do you think murdered Richie Streicher, Mr. LeForge?"

"Lucia has a violent temper. In my judgement, she committed the crime single-handedly."

"A follow-up question. What makes you think so?"

"Just my hunch, that's all."

With that, the questioning ended. Clinton LeForge seemed to have a solid alibi.

The next day, Troopers Collins and Edwards set out to check LeForge's alibi witnesses. First they interviewed Ralph Edwards—no relation to Trooper Edwards. The handyman confirmed he helped LeForge "put up" a new heating stove from two thirty until five fifteen. Edwards added that the only time LeForge left his office was to go to the hardware down the street. He was never gone for more than ten minutes. LeForge paid Edwards fifty cents for helping him that day.

Ypsilanti blacksmith Lewis Smith had little to tell the police. He was in LeForge's office around 5:10 p.m. and left fifteen minutes later. LeForge was there the whole time.

John E. Matthews ran a tin shop next to LeForge's office and stated LeForge came by a couple of times. Matthews remembered lending LeForge a pair of tin snips to modify a stove pipe, but he was unable to cite specific times when LeForge was in his shop.

Next up, the investigators questioned Joseph Diroff—owner and operator of a grocery store on the corner of Michigan Avenue and Park Street. Diroff told the investigators that LeForge picked up empty milk bottles at his store generally between six thirty and seven o'clock most nights. Diroff was unable to confirm LeForge came in that night and had no recollection of LeForge stopping in his shop long enough to listen to the radio.

Troopers Collins and Edwards continued east on Michigan Avenue to the Chamberlain Inn where they interviewed Frank Minni and Mary Wilkie. Minni vouched for LeForge's time on March 7, 1935, from about seven o'clock until sometime between ten thirty and eleven o'clock. Minnie could place the date because LeForge brought them some legal papers to sign. Mary Wilkie remembered LeForge sat with Emory Albertson and a woman. Mary Wilkie didn't know the woman's name.

Ypsilanti patrolman Ernest Rowe also vouched for LeForge's whereabouts at Chamberlain's from seven o'clock until he left at eleven o'clock. Rowe ate dinner with Emory Albertson and Albertson's unnamed lady friend. LeForge came in just like he said, ordered dinner, and sat down with Albertson. Patrolman Rowe hung around the bar waiting for his wife's shift to end. She waitressed at Chamberlain's.

Clinton LeForge appeared to have a strong alibi for March 7th. During the time-frame of Richie's disappearance, LeForge was in his office a half mile away from Depot Town. That's if all the alibi witnesses were telling the truth.

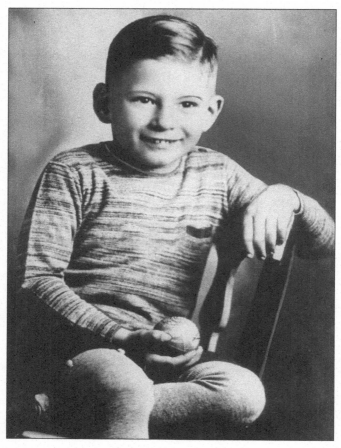

Richard Streicher Jr., kindergarten photo,
age five.

Thirteen-year-old Buck Holt found the body while following muskrat tracks in the snow with his brother Billy.

Buck Holt showing the Ypsilanti Police the body drop site.

Richard Streiche Jr. and class participating in a 1934 Christmas assembly. Richie had only ten more weeks to live.

Ypsilanti Police, 1931. The seated officers all played key roles in the murder investigation. Joseph Sackman, Ernest Klavitter, Ralph Southhard, William Morey, and standing second from the right Ernest Rowe.

Ypsilanti Police dragging the Huron River for the murder weapon. Spectators were kept at bay on the Cross Street Bridge.

Richard Streicher Sr. and his wife Lucia (Mueller) Streicher. Photo credit: The Ypsilanti Daily Press—March 15, 1935.

Lucia Mueller
Pontiac
Camp Fire
Physical Education Club
Physical Education

1928 Aurora yearbook picture of twenty-two-year-old Lucia Mueller in her junior year at Michigan State Normal College. She dropped out in December after the first semester to elope with Richard Streicher Sr. Their son was born on January 27th, 1928.

Clinton LeForge graduation photo from Detroit School of Law in 1908. He is twenty-three years old in this photograph.

The Streicher apartment which faces West Cross Street is the bump out at the rear of the house on North Huron. The Streichers lived there only a few months before the murder of their son.

Depot Town. This photo shows the relative proximity of the Streicher apartment to the Frog Island Bridge (not visible) on the northeast end of the Cross Street Bridge. The Streicher apartment is off-camera to the far left.

Photo credit: Fornology.com

7

Investigation Broadens

After two full weeks of investigation, the Washtenaw County Sheriff's Department, the Ypsilanti Police, and the State Police troopers at the Ypsilanti post were left with innuendo, hunches, and an absence of solid clues. Every shred of evidence and every gossip's rumor was investigated, but local police efforts yielded no hard evidence. The public was alarmed that a young boy could be murdered in daylight on Ypsilanti's second busiest street without someone taking notice. Washtenaw County Sheriff Jacob F. Andres requested assistance from the Michigan State Police in East Lansing. They had a crime lab and were better equipped and trained to investigate homicide than the local police force.

Because of the statewide notoriety of the Streicher case, Michigan governor Frank D. Fitzgerald instructed the state police "to leave no stone unturned in their efforts to help local officials solve this murder." In an all-out effort to recover the murder weapon, authorities arranged to have the Huron River lowered with the help of Superior dam upriver. Both banks and under the Cross Street Bridge were raked over carefully. No knife was found.

On March 18, 1935, Michigan State Police Captain Donald S. Leonard began interviewing people closely connected with the case. The first person interviewed was Mr. Lynn R. Schaffer, the live-in funeral director and embalmer at Moore Funeral Home. Mr. Schaffer said Ypsilanti Police Chief Southard called him at one o'clock on the afternoon of March 8 to pick up a body found under the footbridge off the Cross Street Bridge.

"Mr. Lamb—the crime photographer— was taking photographs of the scene," Schaffer said. "The coroner—Dr. Robb— instructed me to move the body to the funeral home but not embalm it. He ordered an autopsy be performed. We took the boy's frozen body to the funeral home just after two o'clock and placed him on a preparation table."

Captain Leonard showed Schaffer photographs of the boy's body under the bridge. Schaffer confirmed that was how he found the body.

"Was the chin strap of his cap fastened?"

"No."

"What did you do with the boy's clothing?"

"We took it off and put it in a box."

"Who helped?"

"Health Inspector Maddix."

"How did you remove the clothing?"

"By prying and cutting the clothes carefully off the body."

"Why were they cut off?"

"They were frozen. We couldn't get them off any other way."

"Mr. Schaffer, what was done with the clothing?"

"It was placed in a large florist box and set out in the back hall just off the preparation room. As the clothes thawed, water ran all over the wood floor, so we took the box out to the garage and burned the clothes the next day with the waste."

"Anybody instruct you to hold the clothes for evidence?"

"No, we phoned Mrs. Streicher, asking if she wanted her son's clothes back. She told us to burn them. She never wanted to see them again. That Friday night, they were incinerated. When the police inquired about the clothes over the weekend, I told them they were burned up. Investigators sifted through the ashes of the incinerator and found several remnants. Most of the boy's felt-lined cap was recovered, as well as a glove and part of his underwear. The charred remnants were taken to Prosecutor Rapp's office Sunday night."

"Did the boy's parents view their son's body before the autopsy?"

"Neither of them wanted to see him until he was fixed up and laid out in his casket. That was late Saturday night."

Ypsilanti city health inspector, Ernest Maddix, was interviewed next. He reported how Richie Streicher's body was removed from under the footbridge. "We had a shovel. We got one wrist loose, put the shovel under the body, and broke it all out, but one arm was frozen deeper, so I did the rest with my hands."

Captain Leonard asked Maddix if there were any footprints around the crime scene. "There were a lot of people down there—I couldn't tell a thing. Investigators wanted sand spread on the snow, so they could get up and down the slippery bank. That's why we happened to have a shovel handy to pry the body loose. We found no blood pool where the body had been. The victim's clenched hands were frozen inside his mittens, and his clothes and shoes were frozen to his body.

"When the police finished their field investigation, the body was taken to Moore's Funeral Home to thaw. Richie Streicher's stiff clothes were cut from his body and burned at the request of his mother; then I washed the body. The last rites were administered before the autopsy commenced."

———

It was Washtenaw County Coroner Dr. David N. Robb's turn to be questioned by Captain Leonard. "When I arrived on the scene," Robb said, "the body hadn't been disturbed. The boy was found lying on his back on the abutment under the footbridge. His two-piece snowsuit was frozen and looked

wet. There was no pool of water or ice sur-
rounding the body—only the area outlin-
ing the body. The body itself was frozen. I
estimate it took between twelve to fifteen
hours given the ambient air temperature
that evening.

"The body was fully clothed with shirt-tail
and undershirt pulled up on its left side. His
shirttail was tucked inside his pants on his
right side. The boy's jacket was open, but his
pants were fastened. The shirt over his heart
showed some pale evidence of bloodstain.
Both arms were extended outward from his
body. There were no signs of struggle. The
boy had a very composed expression on his
face. After rigor mortis sets in, the expression changes to a more natural appearance."

"After you completed your field examination, what action did you take?"

"I called Moore's Funeral Home to pick
up the body. Then I ordered an autopsy be
performed by Dr. Stacey Howard. I arrived
at the funeral home at nine o'clock that
evening to witness the postmortem. I noticed
the boy's clothes were removed and his body
was cleansed."

"What were Dr. Howard's findings?"

"Of the fourteen wounds found on the body, eight were to the head but not deep enough to penetrate the cranium. We believe the head wounds were made when the Streicher boy was standing. The two superficial slashes found on his throat were not deep enough to cause death or sever his trachea. Of the four wounds on the boy's left chest, three entered his heart. He died within a few seconds after the fatal blows were struck. The attacker didn't need a lot of strength because the knife was very sharp and slender. The incisions were smooth."

Captain Leonard asked one last question. "Is there a possibility that a degenerate mind is at work here, Doctor?"

"Might be" was the coroner's noncommittal answer.

In an effort to prove their innocence and stop the wagging tongues of gossipy neighbors, both Streicher parents agreed to take a series of polygraph tests in April 1935—one month after their son's murder. The polygraph was invented by Professor Leonarde Keeler of Northwestern University and first used in court on February 2, 1935, to convict two criminals. Two months later, it was being used in the Streicher case.

The polygraph measures and records blood pressure, pulse, respiration, and skin conductivity. Variations in physiological responses are recorded by four stylus pens charting the responses simultaneously on a moving roll of graph paper—hence the name polygraph. The popularly accepted belief is that deceptive answers will record different responses than true answers. All questions require a simple yes-or-no answer. A normal response is first established by asking the test subject several innocuous questions to record a baseline response—then questions about the crime are asked to gauge any differences in response on the part of the subject.

Richard Streicher Sr. underwent his polygraph tests at Michigan State Police headquarters in East Lansing on April 17. He was given six separate tests with inter-rogation between tests. Mr. Streicher coop-erated in every possible way. Polygraph tests are privileged information and specific questions and responses are not released to the public. His responses showed some mass reaction on his graph chart but no spikes indicating guilt or further knowledge of his son's murder.

The following week, Lucia went to East Lansing for her battery of polygraph tests and interrogations. State police chief of detectives Van A. Loomis reported to the media that she pleaded with them to question her as though they actually believed she had killed her child. "Let the lie detector show that I'm telling the truth," Mrs. Streicher said. Lucia wept as she spoke of rumor mongering and finger-pointing by people who were once her friends. As with her husband, Lucia showed some mass reaction throughout the tests. Examiner Sergeant Harold Mulbar was of the opinion that this was due to a nervous reaction; however, her graph chart showed no specific responses or spiking to questions concerning the murder of her son.

Polygraph examiner Sergeant Mulbar had never met Mrs. Streicher, but he formed the opinion that she had a "close to border-line psychopathic condition." He said, "This may be the result of shock over the brutal murder of her son or that she has been the victim of malicious rumors that point suspicion her way. She may have brought this situation upon herself in regard to her numerous prevarications in connection with this case." Sergeant Mulbar believed both parents could have given further information, but there was no hard indication either was lying.

Later that same month, Clinton LeForge was brought in for polygraph testing and interrogation in East Lansing. LeForge was then under indictment for embezzlement to the tune of $3,685 from the estate of Darwin Z. Curtis in Northern Michigan. He was questioned only about the murder. His polygraph showed some mass reaction to the questions generally, and Sergeant Mulbar believed there was some indication Clinton LeForge might be withholding information that could be of value in the investigation, but there were no specifics as to what that information might be.

Polygraph tests measure arousal and are inherently subjective. They can be affected by anxiety disorders and other factors. Cunning people have been known to defeat them. In 2002 the National Research Council noted, "There is no specific physiological reaction associated with lying. The mechanisms associated with lying are unknown, making it difficult to identify factors that separate liars from truth tellers." The National Academy of Sciences' position on the accuracy of polygraph tests is they "are simply unreliable, unscientific, biased, and inadmissible in the United States court system." But during the Great Depression, polygraph tests—popularly known as lie detector tests—were on the cutting edge of crime-fighting technology. Passing the polygraph tests bolstered the Streichers' claims of innocence.

———————

At the end of May, 1935, the Michigan attorney general sent assistants Albert Wing and James Stewart to interview the Streichers in Grand Rapids, where the Streichers were staying because of unwelcomed notoriety in Ypsilanti. Richard Streicher had secured a tool and die job there. With the investigators was psychologist Dr. P. C. Robertson from Ionia State (mental) Hospital to observe the Streichers under questioning. Dr. Robertson was introduced simply as a member of the attorney general's staff and did not participate in the questioning.

The investigators asked Lucia Streicher to recount the story of her son's disappearance one more time. By this time, her responses were well-rehearsed and consistent with previous statements. The attorney general's investigators asked Lucia if her son had any pineapple cake on the day of his murder. She admitted baking a pineapple cake a few days before Richie disappeared, but she threw the cake out because it had dried out. Lucia insisted her son did not eat any cake the day he went missing. When asked how he could have undigested pineapple in his stomach, she answered, "The only possible explanation must be he ate some pineapple in Jell-O or something at school."

Investigators asked Lucia who she now thought committed the murder after the people she previously accused were found innocent. Without hesitation, she said Fred Leighton, the hatchery man. This was Lucia's first mention of Leighton to investigators. Police had cleared Frederick Leighton in an earlier investigation, but Lucia insisted the police were not thorough enough. How she knew this was anybody's guess.

Richard Streicher Sr. was also questioned by the attorney general's investigators when he got home from his job. Despite several reports to the contrary, the Streichers were living together. Lucia was present for his interview. Richard stated that after work on the day Richie went missing, he returned home at about four-thirty. The rest of his recollection of that evening was remarkably similar to his wife's version, except he added that he brought Richie's sled inside when he found it leaning against the house. The sled's runners were turned away from the house which was different than how Richie always left his sled with the runners leaning against the house. When questioned about the pineapple cake, Richard stated Richie did not have any on the day he went missing. Investigators must have wondered how Richard could be so certain when he spent the day working, but they did not press him.

In a debriefing session after both interviews, Dr. Robertson told the investigators that from his observations, he did not believe either of the Streichers was complicit in their son's murder. Robertson agreed Frederick Leighton needed greater scrutiny—another hard-won point for the Streichers.

On September 16, 1935, seven months after the Streicher murder, Washtenaw County Prosecutor Albert J. Rapp informed a press conference, "Thus far, all efforts to solve this crime have been without avail. I have made the decision to exhume Richard Streicher Jr.'s body in the hope of finding new evidence to verify or eliminate various theories formulated by police."

As caretakers from Highland Cemetery started the disinterment, police guards were placed at the entrance of the cemetery to prevent visitors from witnessing the gruesome sight. The coffin was taken immediately to the basement morgue of the University of Michigan Hospital where a thorough autopsy was performed that evening. Washtenaw County Coroner Dr. Buegher was looking for details not documented in the first examination, in particular broken bones, skull fractures, and the contents of the boy's stomach to determine if he was poisoned. All the law enforcement commanders working this case were present in the gallery as witnesses.

The casket was opened. Richie was clothed in a white linen suit with white shoes and short white stockings. He had a Mickey Mouse watch on his left wrist and a signet ring on his left-hand ring finger. The body was photographed clothed before being undressed. Subsequent photographs were taken of the naked body to compare with photographs from the original autopsy.

The body was in an advanced state of putrid decomposition "with heavy growth of mold over all the exposed surfaces but markedly around the face and extremities. The face was covered in fungus and the eyes were sunken in their orbits. The teeth were all present but very loose in their sockets."

After a thorough examination, the coroner found no signs of skeletal fractures or bruising suggesting a struggle. Richie's neck had not been broken. Shreds of pineapple and fat globules were found in the boy's stomach. Upon further investigation, it was discovered that Jell-O with whipped cream was served for lunch at Richie's school the afternoon he went missing. Cafeteria staff could not verify if there was pineapple in the Jell-O or not, but it was irrelevant. Dr. Buegher confirmed Richie was not poisoned.

The first autopsy done by Dr. Howard suggested that the puncture wounds on the chest revealed the murder weapon was "a slender, double-edged knife like a stiletto." Upon closer examination, the second autopsy showed the wounds to be clean cut on one side. This suggested a single-edged weapon with a tapered end like a household kitchen knife or a pair of sewing shears. Dr. Buegher took some shears, opened them, and stabbed another cadaver in the morgue to see if the wounds resembled the wounds on the boy's body. They did—particularly the eight cranial wounds.

Richie's body was returned to Highland Cemetery and reburied before daybreak. On October 9, 1935, Prosecutor Rapp announced that Dr. Buegher's final report on the examination yielded no new information—another frustrating outcome for investigators.

— 8 —

Scapegoating

When the inquiry into the murder of their son was reopened, the Streichers voluntarily submitted to truth serum tests, hoping to convince the police and the public of their innocence. Sodium pentothal was invented in 1934 as a sedative or painkiller but was soon found to relax subjects who would answer questions in an unguarded fashion while under its influence.

On November 9, 1935, Dr. Raymond W. Waggoner—head of the Neuropsychopathic Institute of the University of Michigan Hospital—administered the serum to each parent in separate interviews. Only partial excerpts from Lucia's transcript were available from the Michigan State Police, and no transcript for Richard's test was found.

Lucia was questioned by Lieutenant L.W. Morse.

Q—Who killed Richard?

A—The hatchery man. Get him and give him the works.

Q—When was the last time you saw your son, Richard?

A—At about five fifteen on the front lawn.

Q—Was anyone with him?

A—No, he was alone playing—seemed to be having a good time.

Q—Have you talked to Clinton LeForge since Richard's death?

A—Yes, he came to the apartment and packed up Richard's toys.

Q—Did you lose a knife?

A—No.

Q—Have you got any knives?

A—Yes, three.

Q—Where are they?

A—Gone. You don't think I would have them after you stuck them into cadavers.

Q—Did you bake a pineapple cake on the day Richard went missing?

A—No, it was the Monday before.

Q—Did Richard eat any of the cake on the day he disappeared?

A—No, I don't think so.

Q—Did Clinton LeForge kill Richard?

A—No, my in-laws know who killed him.

Q—Why was Richard killed?

A—Can't tell?

Q—Who put Richard under the foot-bridge?

A—Don't know. The hatchery man does.

Q—Did your husband do it?

A—No.

Q—Who do you think killed Richard?

A—My father-in-law and the hatchery man.

This line of questioning went no place contributing nothing new to the case. Absolutely no link could be established between the Streicher elder and Frederick Leighton, much less a conspiracy to murder an innocent seven-year-old boy.

Both Streichers implicated Leighton in their son's disappearance and murder for three reasons. First, Richie was known to go into the hatchery from time to time; second, Leighton allegedly promised Richie a baby chick; and third, Lucia ran into Leighton on the bridge at seven o'clock the morning after Richie went missing. Leighton asked if she had found her boy. How did he know that early in the morning her son was missing?

Sixty-two-year-old Frederick Leighton, manager of the Neuhauser Chicken Hatchery just down the street from the Streicher apartment was requestioned by Albert Wing and James Stewart from the Attorney General's Office, along with Lieutenant Detective Philip L. Hutson of the Michigan State Police. Leighton told investigators the Streicher boy would often play back and forth in front of the hatchery but was not in the habit of coming into the place. "And he wasn't there on March seventh."

When asked if he ever promised to give Richie a baby chick, Leighton said, "The only time I spoke to the boy about giving him a chick was when he was in my shop with his mother. The kid asked me, 'Would you give me a chick?' I said, 'Did I promise you one?' That was it!"

"When did you first learn about Richard's disappearance?"

"About six o'clock Friday morning when I was at the gas station. Old man Anderson told me."

"Would you consent to a polygraph test?"

"Only under certain conditions," Leighton answered. "First, my lawyer has to consent, and second, Prosecutor Rapp needs to be a witness to correct false accusations made against my name. It's bad for business."

Leighton's lawyer advised his client to put this matter behind him as fast as he could. Leighton agreed to take the polygraph test but not in Lansing. Arrangements were made to give him the test in a room at the Huron Hotel in Ypsilanti. After several tests, it was determined Leighton "showed no specific responses to questions pertaining to this crime, which indicates no guilty knowledge." Leighton was cleared as a suspect, much to the chagrin of Lucia Streicher.

Five months had passed since Richie's body was found. Ypsilanti Police Chief Ralph Southard, Washtenaw County Sheriff Andres, and Washtenaw County Prosecuting Attorney Albert R. Rapp were all of the opinion that Lucia Streicher killed or was complicit in her son's murder. All they lacked was hard evidence to prove it.

On August 12, 1935, self-professed psychic Mrs. Fred Gordon contacted Chief Southard saying she read about the murder in the Detroit papers, and she could tell if Mrs. Streicher was guilty of the crime. Placing no faith in fortune-tellers but wanting to leave no stone unturned, the chief sent Corporal Frank Walker and E. L. Squires, a civilian investigator for the Ford Motor Company's Security Department, to ask Lucia if she would be interested in a tarot card or crystal ball reading from Mrs. Gordon. Lucia agreed only if the police would pay because she was short of funds and had little faith in such nonsense.

The investigators met with Mrs. Gordon in Ecorse Township in what is now Taylor, Michigan, about twenty-three miles east of Ypsilanti. They paid her fifty dollars cash— not a bad sum for the Great Depression. That evening, Walker and Squires drove both Streichers to Mrs. Gordon's home. Lucia Streicher met with Mrs. Gordon from seven thirty until nine o'clock while the three men waited outside. When Lucia returned to the car, she was visibly disturbed and asked to get away from there immediately. After some protracted sobbing, Lucia was able to speak, and she told Walker and Squires what the psychic told her.

In Squire's report to Prosecutor Rapp, he wrote that Lucia told them the psychic revealed her son was in the basement of the hatchery and was killed by a man who worked there. She described the man as around fifty years old with thinning, reddish-gray hair. The psychic further claimed that in her vision, Lucia's son was playing with some baby chicks in the hatchery basement and was discovered. The man struck Richie and pushed him away from the hatchling trays. Richie hit his head on the end of a table and was knocked out. When Richie did not regain consciousness, the hatchery man panicked. He stabbed the boy to make it look like a degenerate killed him. He wrapped the boy's body in a blanket, carried the bundle up the basement stairs, and then the hatchery man sneaked it under the Cross Street Bridge. He waded across the Huron River and placed the body under the footbridge. The man buried the knife along the riverbank. The psychic's vision was remarkably detailed and polished—as told by Lucia. Investigators showed particular interest in one detail they could follow up on—the buried knife.

After Corporal Walker and Squires returned the Streichers to Ypsilanti, they went back to talk with Mrs. Gordon about the knife. The psychic said she was confident she could find the knife and point out the murderer. Walker convinced Mrs. Gordon to go to Ypsilanti the next morning to take a look at Fred Leighton and find the knife. On August 15th, she came to the Ypsilanti police station with her husband. Under police protection, they went to the hatchery to take a look at Fred Leighton. Mrs. Gordon said she identified Leighton as the man she saw in her vision. Leighton was understandably upset with the Gordons and the police.

That evening, Walker and Squires rolled up to the Gordon house, surprised to discover the Streichers there. The investigators waited until they left at about eleven o'clock, then Walker and Squires knocked on the front door. Mrs. Gordon was caught off guard. Without being invited into the house, they asked Gordon if she would return to Ypsilanti at nine o'clock the next morning to show them where the knife was buried. She reluctantly agreed, only after Corporal Walker convinced her the police would lure Leighton away from the hatchery and pay her for her time. Mrs. Gordon said she feared reprisals. Walker assured her officers would pick Leighton up before nine o'clock and bring him to the station for fingerprinting and questioning taking at least an hour.

The psychic agreed to be at the hatchery at the appointed time, but she was a no-show. Frustrated, the police drove to the Gordon house, but she was not home. A neighbor said she left to go shopping in Detroit and wouldn't be back until later.

Sergeant Walker contacted Lucia Streicher by phone to see if she knew anything. Lucia told Walker that she spoke with Gordon over the phone. Gordon told Lucia she was afraid the police would cross her up under the current arrangement, and Mrs. Gordon's husband told her not to get further involved. It became apparent the Streichers and the Gordons were conspiring to set up Leighton to take the murder rap.

Corporal Walker and Squires returned the following day and found Mrs. Gordon at home. They asked her to tell them the truth, or they would be forced to take her to Ypsilanti for further questioning. Gordon thought it best to cooperate. She told investigators that Lucia was contemplating leaving her husband and going with another man—a reputed underworld figure who wanted to open a gambling house in Ecorse Township. Lucia was under the impression that she was going to help run the operation, but she needed a thousand dollars right away and needed to put the finger on Fred Leighton. There was a reward for the arrest and conviction of her son's slayer. Gordon said Lucia let slip the remark, "I made a huge mistake. My husband should have been killed instead of my son." The investigators took the "psychic's" remarks under advisement but placed no great stock in her information.

9

Conspiracy to Obstruct Justice

With public opinion running heavily against her and believing Prosecutor Rapp was about to indict her, Lucia was desperate to frame Frederick Leighton for her son's murder. But the Ypsilanti Police had questioned and cleared him twice. What Lucia needed more than anything was a confession signed by him.

After Lucia's neighbor Frances Weimar was seen leaving the Streicher apartment one afternoon, the police followed her home for a chat. Weimar offered a sympathetic ear to Lucia and was the only neighbor Lucia still spoke with or invited into her apartment. Both ladies shared an interest in pulp mystery and crime magazines. Weimar proved to be a talkative subject. She told police, "Lucia isn't really separated from her husband. Richard is keeping an eye on the Ypsi police, and she's doing the same in Ann Arbor." That information went a long way to explain why the Streichers were able to keep their stories straight—even when interviewed separately.

Weimar added that while visiting the Streicher apartment, Lucia asked Richard about kidnapping Fred Leighton. "Lucia wanted to know if it was better to stand trial on a murder charge rather that a kidnapping charge. She was afraid of the Lindberg Law. Richard told her kidnapping carried a federal death penalty, but murder in Michigan only carried a life sentence." When police asked Weimar if she thought Lucia was guilty of murdering her son, Weimar said she wasn't certain. Even Lucia's last friend had her doubts.

Traditional investigative channels produced little result, so Prosecutor Rapp engineered a cloak and dagger plan to catch Lucia making an incriminating statement. Frances Weimar agreed to cooperate with the prosecutor's plan to covertly record Lucia Streicher conversation in the Leland Hotel in downtown Detroit. What inducement Rapp brought to bear to make her a willing pawn is unknown. Perhaps Weimar wanted to satisfy her own curiosity. She considered herself an amateur sleuth. Now she was part of an authentic sting operation.

Weimar told Lucia she had the phone number of an underworld figure who might be willing to help get a confession out of Leighton. Lucia was running out of options. Expecting a pending indictment at any time, she dialed Jack Miller's number and told him a friend gave her his number. Lucia said she was hoping he might be able to help her. A clandestine meeting was arranged for October 11, 1935, at the Leland Hotel in downtown Detroit.

The Streichers didn't own a car, so Frances Weimar volunteered to drive Lucia the thirty-six miles into Detroit. To establish an alibi and justify the trip, Weimar told her husband she and Lucia were going downtown to the Cass Theater to see a live performance of *Tobacco Road*. Weimar paid four dollars for the tickets.

Before the play, Lucia and Frances walked to the Leland Hotel and went to room 803 as directed by Jack Miller. Miller acted surprised to see Frances Weimar with Lucia, but Lucia assured him that Frances was her trusted friend. With Miller was another man in the room who introduced himself as Al Helicher.

Most of this meeting and a subsequent meeting were recorded on the plastic cylinders of a Dictograph recorder setup in room 802, connected by wires to room 803. The recording cylinders of the Dictograph had to be changed every fifteen minutes, so there are brief gaps in the conversation. Sometimes the microphones did not pick up everything, and sometimes the transcriptions were sketchy. The wires were hidden under the carpeting connecting two microphones nestled under the table where the four persons sat and talked.

Readers may wonder why gangsters would record a meeting about kidnapping that could provide incriminating evidence against them. Detroit underworld figures Miller and Helicher were actually Wayne County Deputy Sheriffs Howard Heinrich and Alfred E. Farrell working undercover on behalf of the Washtenaw County prosecutor. Because Lucia was familiar with most of the Washtenaw County police, Prosecutor Rapp chose to farm out the clandestine operation to Wayne County. The authorities were as desperate to prove their case against Lucia as she was to prove her innocence. The prosecutor hoped for anything to tumble the house of cards that was Lucia's defense.

After Lucia briefed Miller and Helicher on her narrative of the facts, she told them she believed the police and the prosecutor in Washtenaw County were afraid of Fred Leighton, so she had to take measures into her own hands.

"Captain Marmon of the state police gave me seventy-two hours of unmolested time to get the man to sign a confession. For my part, I told them I would either bring in the missing knife or get Fred Leighton to confess. After seventy-two hours, I have to report to the district attorney. We've got to get a signed confession tonight."

Jack Miller (Officer Howard Heinrich) asked, "How are you going to get a confession?"

"Don't ask me! I was hoping you could help me."

"I don't know how the hell a guy could do that to a kid. If you want us to get this guy, we got to know why he done it. What do you know about this guy who killed your kid?"

"I know he has a forgery charge against him and he beats his wife. I've been running around in circles for the last five months. The police know Leighton has a violent temper," Lucia said. "Fred Leighton killed Richie."

Miller responded, "Al and me could help you, but that puts us on the spot."

"I can get a confession out of Leighton. He knows where the knife is hidden."

Al Helicher (Officer Alfred E. Farrell) spoke for the first time. "Why couldn't the police find the knife?"

"They were looking in the wrong place."

"How the hell do we know that's true? Why didn't you point out where the knife was to the police?"

"They would have taken that for my guilt. I haven't done a damned thing. The prosecutor can't pin anything on me. I can get the hatchery man to confess."

"If you would come clean with us, maybe we could help you," Miller said.

"A woman I know told police Leighton buried the knife along the riverbank."

"What woman?"

Lucia was unresponsive and grimaced.

After an awkward silence, Weimar interjected, "The fortune-teller."

"The what? You've got us in hell of a mess."

"The police gave me the name of a psychic in Ecorse Township. After I met with her, I went to the police with the facts."

"As told to you by a fortune-teller?"

"I didn't do it, Jack. Fred Leighton is the kind of man the police are afraid of."

"Why is that?"

"They are afraid he'll sue them for false arrest."

"What's going to happen if we bring this guy in?" Helicher asked.

"I think he'll confess. Why does Leighton go around town telling people he did it, but when he sees me coming down the street, he ducks into a doorway or alley?"

"Maybe he's afraid you'll do him next."

"Thank you, Jack. You think I'm guilty too, don't you?"

"I don't know. You're so goddamned sure somebody else did it. If you could only let down with some facts. What if we take this guy for a ride and he's the wrong guy?"

"There's no one else it could be."

"That's what you say. Why would the hatchery man incriminate himself? It doesn't make sense. Who did Leighton tell?"

"People in Ypsilanti."

"Any names?"

"No, I just heard rumors."

"You're being evasive again," Helicher said. "Without proof, rumors carry no weight in court. Mrs. Streicher, Jack and me might be able to help you, but you've got to come clean with us. Kidnapping is a serious matter. It's a federal rap. We've got to blow town next week. We're putting ourselves on the spot for you and don't want to run into any difficulties."

"Get Leighton and take me to him. I'll accuse him to his face. I'm not afraid of him. The state police say if they can get the knife, they can get the man."

"You want us to force the man to find the knife. Why can't you just show the police if you know where the knife is?"

"The Ypsilanti police lowered the river level to search the bottom for that knife, but they found nothing. Leighton insists he doesn't know anything about the knife."

"Why are you so sure he does?"

"He described the knife."

"Did he? To whom?" Miller asked.

"I don't know. That's what the Ypsi police told me."

"Which officer told you that?"

"I don't know his name. One of the Ypsi cops."

"That's pretty vague. If Leighton is innocent as he claims, why would he incriminate himself in public? It doesn't make sense," Helicher said.

"I don't know. Investigator Lynn Squires found a letter opener in my house and tried to frame me. I never saw the letter opener before."

"How is that relevant? Did the letter opener match your son's wounds?" Helicher asked.

"I don't know. The police didn't let me see the wounds."

"Who told you about the wounds?"

"The police showed me photographs. Don't you think I know why they showed me those pictures? To see if I would break down. They believed if I was guilty, I'd break. I'm telling you, if I was guilty, I couldn't stand all this."

"That isn't proof, Mrs. Streicher."

"Jack, if I wanted to kill any member of my family, my husband would have taken the bullet. I can't get my divorce until the crime is solved."

"Do you think your husband's people had anything to do with it?"

"I think they wanted to but didn't have the nerve."

"How can we help you if you don't come clean with us?"

"I haven't done anything the prosecutor can pin on me. I absolutely didn't do it."

"You say you know where the knife is. How do you know that?"

"A woman saw the hatchery man bury the knife."

"What woman?"

"I can't tell you."

"Why not?"

"She's afraid of reprisals."

"So, here we go again. Did the fortune-teller give the police the location of the knife?"

Frances Weimar spoke up. "Lou, are you sure she saw the guy bury the knife?"

"Yes, in her vision, but the police didn't dig where she said."

"Why the hell not?" Miller said losing his patience.

"Because the police can't see anyone else guilty but the lawyer or me."

"Maybe they figured the ground was too frozen to dig into the banks," said Helicher.

"I didn't kill my son," she implored. "Absolutely not! I have no motive."

"How does freedom sound as a motive?"

"Freedom? Freedom from what?"

"Your marriage, so you could run away with the lawyer."

"I won't dignify that with an answer, Jack."

"Why did you come down here today, Mrs. Streicher?"

"Not to argue or be accused of murdering my son, that's for certain."

"What's to worry about if you're innocent? Nobody ever worried unless they had a guilty conscience."

"I didn't do it. If we can get the hatchery man, I'm telling you, he'll confess."

"Why hasn't he been charged for this crime?"

"Prosecutor Rapp is a coward and would rather harass a poor woman than confront Leighton."

"The prosecutor can't arrest anyone without evidence." Miller put more pressure on Lucia. "You're telling too goddamned much and don't know anything, or you know everything and you're trying to cover it up. Which is it, Mrs. Streicher?"

"Don't be so hard-boiled, Jack."

"Why don't you wise up and tell us what you know? Don't waste our time. I don't give a good goddamn about this. I could be ocean fishing right now. What the hell did you come down here for?"

"We thought you could help her," Weimar interjected.

"What about your husband, Mrs. Streicher? Did he have anything to do with the murder? I read in the newspaper that you accused him and his family," Helicher said.

"No, he didn't! But my husband should have had the works done to him instead of Junior. I've thought many times of ending it all myself, but if I did, that son of a bitch would say, 'Aha! She couldn't take it.'"

"Why don't you just get it over with?" Helicher continued. "Prove your innocence in court and be done with it."

"If you think I'm returning to face a murder rap, you're screwy."

"I'm going down to Florida next week, and I don't want to get in a jam. Why the dirty look?"

"I thought you could help me, Jack."

"I can if you give us the straight dope."

"You two don't believe me, do you?"

"There's something missing, Mrs. Streicher."

"Yes, there is—the hatchery man's confession."

Miller threw Lucia a bone. "Okay, we'll roust Leighton to see what we can find out. Meet us back here in a couple of days. We'll contact you. Don't leave us hanging."

"I won't. That would make me look guilty."

"Yes, it would," Miller said.

The first Dictograph interview ended and was transcribed for examination by the prosecutor and investigators. The next day, Ypsilanti police pulled Fred Leighton out of the Martha Washington movie theater for further questioning. Authorities were more convinced than ever that Leighton had nothing to do with Streicher murder.

After Leighton's interrogation, the undercover officers returned to the Leland Hotel on October 14 to report their findings to Mrs. Streicher. The room was still wired for sound. This time, Jack Miller and Al Helicher left the ladies alone in the room for a time, hoping Lucia might reveal something incriminating in an unguarded moment. The women said nothing about the case, so the undercover police returned to place more pressure on Lucia.

"Mrs. Streicher, we're holding Fred Leighton at an undisclosed location," Miller began. "But we need to let him go soon. Understand?"

"What did he say, Jack?"

"He talked plenty."

"Yes, what did he say?"

"You know goddamned well Leighton didn't have anything to do with the murder."

"He did too!"

"Who implicated this guy in the first place?"

"I can't tell you."

"Was it the fortune-teller or other people?"

"Other people."

"Leighton points the finger at you and the lawyer, claiming you and Dick are goddamned liars looking for a scapegoat. He says he can place you right in the middle."

"And you believe him? I told you all I know. That lawyer blew town because he embezzled eighteen hundred dollars (sic)."

"All right, what else do you know?"

"Nothing, I swear."

"Your friend is sitting here with a silly goddamn grin on her face. Do you two know the gravity of the situation? Kidnapping is a capital offense. We're not playing games."

"Certainly, we do."

"Do you understand what's going to happen to this guy if there's a slipup?"

"I imagine the police will find his body somewhere. Get him out of the state if you do that."

"Get serious! You were running around with LeForge. Admit it!"

"No, I wasn't!"

"That's not what Leighton says."

"He is a damned liar." Lucia turned and addressed her friend. "All right, Fran, was I running around with the lawyer or not?"

Chastened, Frances Weimar answered, "I don't know if you and Clinton had a date, Lucia. I don't know anything about it. I'm sorry." Weimar may not have wanted to perjure herself.

"Your story keeps changing, Mrs. Streicher."

"Maybe you have bad information."

"Did you ever go out with the lawyer?"

"No, I was in his apartment one time."

"If you want us to help you..."

"What? Lie about something that isn't so? There isn't a damn thing I can tell you. Who do you think did it?"

Jack Miller was smart enough not to accuse Mrs. Streicher directly. "I'm going to shove off tomorrow," he said. "We need to release Leighton before we get caught up on a kidnapping charge."

"Mrs. Streicher, one last time, what do you know about Clinton LeForge?"

"LeForge was going to represent me in a divorce proceeding. When Richie died, my husband and I changed our minds. That's it!"

"We have to cut Leighton loose."

"Never!" Lucia demanded. "I'll kill the guy before I let him go. I know goddamned well he killed my son. Fred Leighton is guilty as hell. Is your gun registered, Jack?"

"No."

"Give me your gun and take me where you're holding him."

"Not a chance. Leighton begged us to turn him over to the police."

"Sure, the guy's smart. He wants the dough. He thinks he's a big shot."

"Leighton points the finger at you and the lawyer. If you are guilty, he'll get the reward."

"He'll break sooner or later. I told you he wouldn't break in a few hours."

"What about your lawyer friend, Mrs. Streicher?"

"I told you I haven't seen that goddamned lawyer since 1933."

"Earlier you mentioned LeForge wanted you to divorce Dick and marry him."

"I never said that. Maybe Fran told you that."

"I didn't say that, Lucia."

"Didn't you tell us a couple of days ago that Clinton LeForge wanted to marry you?"

"Well, he suggested it once."

"You know LeForge is married, don't you?"

Lucia sat silent.

"LeForge removed your son's toys from his room the day after your boy was found. True?"

"I guess so."

"That had to be March of 1935. You just claimed you haven't seen LeForge since 1933?"

"I misspoke. I'm upset."

"How do you know the hatchery man did it?"

"Leighton was the only person with opportunity."

"You told us the first time we spoke that you thought the lawyer might be guilty."

"Someone else told you that."

"No! You told us that." Miller laid on the pressure while Helicher kept a steady stare on Lucia.

"If the lawyer did it, then I'm just as guilty as he is. I said I didn't do it."

"Where is LeForge?"

"In Mexico."

"Who told you that?"

"Prosecutor Rapp."

"You know what I'm thinking, Lucia? You're trying to shield LeForge. You're afraid to tell us things?"

"No, for crying out loud, the prosecutor told me LeForge was in Mexico."

"Prosecutor Rapp?"

"Yes."

"Before God, if there is anything you know, tell me now."

"Take me to the hatchery man, and I'll confront him."

"Leighton claims the lawyer did it, and you know all about it."

"He's a damned liar. Let him prove it!"

"Why are you so sure your lawyer friend didn't do it?"

"I don't know. He just didn't."

"That's pretty vague. Why are you so sure Leighton killed your boy? Do you have any facts?"

"Are you telling me Leighton didn't come across?"

"I've been telling you that for the last thirty minutes. Leighton places the blame directly on you and LeForge."

"You think I would kill my own child?"

"You're a suspect."

"No, I'm not!"

"Prove it! Al and I went out on a limb for you. We need facts, not opinions."

"You're not going to get any more out of me. The Ypsilanti Police think I'm guilty, just like you do. You know there will be a warrant for my arrest when I return to Ypsi, don't you?"

"We don't know that. What are your options, Mrs. Streicher?"

"I'm not sure. I guess the only thing for me to do is go back and face the music."

"Are you going to tell the prosecutor you're guilty?"

"I told you I didn't do it."

"In my language, 'face the music' means you admit guilt."

"I'm not guilty. But if I can't bring in the knife or the hatchery man's confession, I'll have to take the rap, I guess."

"Good luck, Mrs. Streicher. There's nothing we can do for you. Goodbye."

With that, the undercover officers left the room, leaving the Dictaphone still recording the conversation between Lucia and Francis.

Weimar asked, "If you did it, Lucia, why don't you stand trial and plead insanity?"

"Even you think I did it. I didn't do it, Fran."

"Well, if you plead insanity, they would only hold you for one year."

"Only one year? After I regained my sanity, I'd have to stand trial. Then, I'd have to take the rap anyway. No, Leighton has to confess. We're going to pin it on him."

"You're going to pin it on him. But how?"

"I don't know."

"Let's go home, Lucia."

"I'm not going back to Ypsi tonight. I can't go back."

Even with the undercover cops gone from the room, Lucia did not let her guard down for a moment, but she was clearly disturbed waiting for the other shoe to drop.

— 10 —

To Prosecute or Not

In an attempt to consolidate evidence and determine whether the county had an actionable case against the Streichers, Prosecutor Rapp's office summarized a number of questions based on interviews with the Streichers that needed answers.

On the day the Streichers were notified of their son's murder—and for five days afterward—why were the parents so insistent they both be present when either was questioned? They were inseparable. Since then, the Streichers have been separated and questioned many times alone, yet they always know what the other was questioned about, down to the smallest detail. Why are the Streichers comparing notes? For mutual protection?

On the day Richie went missing, Captain Marmon asked Richard Streicher if his son was in the habit of coming home late. Streicher said he was, but they usually knew where to find him. But up to this incident, the parents had never borrowed a car to search for their son. Why did they respond with such urgency on this occasion?

The Streichers were known to quarrel violently over money. Mr. Streicher complains he can't sleep at night due to quarrels with Lucia over money. He describes her as emotional, nervous, and unstable. Several neighbors reported that Richard came home from work at five thirty on the day Richie went missing, and he and Lucia quarreled violently. Why do both parents deny this?

Mrs. Streicher has admitted her unfaithfulness in the presence of her husband. Mr. Streicher knows she had sexual relations with Clinton LeForge and says he no longer loves his wife. Lucia Streicher openly declared her intention to get a divorce, and her husband had no objections. Clinton LeForge represented Mrs. Streicher in a divorce action. Why didn't the Streichers go through with it? What is the bond binding them together?

Both parents have violent tempers as verified by family and neighbors. Clinton LeForge also spoke of Lucia's temper. Several eyewitnesses report that Lucia was known to slap Richie in the face which her husband confirmed. How much violence was Richie Streicher subjected to in the home? Richie was last known to be going home to warm up at four thirty. Did Richie ever leave the apartment alive?

Why did Lucia have LeForge take the boy's toys away? The normal response of a grieving mother would be to leave the child's room and things the way he left them. After LeForge left with the toys, Lucia asked her husband to check inside a box in their bedroom to see if LeForge had planted a knife inside. Richard denied Lucia asked him to check inside a box. What was her motive to lie?

Within the first week of her son's murder, Lucia Streicher accused six different people of her son's murder. Is this Lucia's way of diverting suspicion away from herself? It only draws attention to herself and makes her look guilty.

Lucia waited until early October before she mentioned following footprints in the snow leading to the chicken hatchery. None of the officers assigned to the case had ever heard Lucia mention Frederick Leighton or the Neuhauser Chicken Hatchery down the street from their apartment. Why did she withhold this evidence for six months?

Lucia now insists the hatchery man is guilty, despite not knowing him or having any tangible proof. Even after inquiries cleared Leighton of any involvement in Richie's murder, Lucia still insists he is the man. During a secretly recorded interview, Lucia urged two undercover police to use any method necessary to get Leighton to confess. She is heard to say, "Give me your gun, and I'll get a confession out of him." Why is Lucia so desperate for a scapegoat when a verifiable alibi would clear her?

The lethal wounds on Richie's chest occurred between the third interspace of his ribcage, suggesting someone with knowledge of anatomy placed them there. According to her husband, Lucia had some premed training at Ypsilanti Normal School while preparing to become a physical education teacher. Three out of the four thrusts pierced the boy's heart without nicking the ribs. No unusual strength was needed to drive the knife home. As far as investigators can determine, the boy's mother is the only suspect with this specialized knowledge.

Lucia stated to police that the assailant was left-handed while she and her husband were right-handed. Dr. Buegher's autopsy report clearly states the placement of the head and neck wounds show conclusively that the assailant was right-handed. What makes Lucia insist the killer was left-handed? It isn't consistent with the evidence.

From the undigested contents of the boy's stomach, Dr. Buegher's autopsy report indicates shreds of pineapple. This evidence set the time of death between four thirty and six thirty--five to seven hours after Richie's noon school lunch. Lucia Streicher admits baking a pineapple cake on the sixth of March but insists her son never ate any. When asked what happened to the cake, Lucia said she threw it away a couple of days after Richie's murder because it was stale.

After seven months of investigation, the police and the prosecutor had more questions than answers. Law enforcement was no closer to solving this murder than they were the day Richard Streicher Jr. was discovered under the Frog Island Bridge.

Criminal investigation agencies during the Depression had no DNA registries, national crime databases, networked computers, security cameras, or even social security numbers to track a person. Whoever committed Richie's murder had out maneuvered law enforcement. That was certain. During the Depression, it was still possible to simply disappear.

Captain I. H. Marmon at the Michigan State Police post in Ann Arbor wrote a letter to Commander Oscar G. Olander at the East Lansing post, describing the five hours he spent questioning Mrs. Streicher on the sixteenth of October.

"Mrs. Streicher says so many things, none can be taken seriously. She refuses to make any statement to Prosecutor Rapp. She has accused her husband, her in-laws, Clinton LeForge, John Testo, and Fred Leighton; then she changes her mind and says anyone could have done it.

"The Streichers were alleged to be separated and in fear of each other, but they get together and compare notes after we question them. Coroner Dr. Buegher said in his judgment, the stabbing to the heart was done by someone with knowledge of anatomy. None of the suspects except Mrs. Streicher has studied anatomy."

———————

In a brief to Prosecutor Rapp written by an unattributed investigator after the Dictaphone interviews, the writer focuses mainly on Lucia Streicher and Clinton LeForge—the prime suspects. The informality and unprofessional tone of the fourteen-page report is fraught with ambiguity and a lack of hard evidence further compromised by the investigator's opinion and personal bias. This document alone would be enough to support the belief that the investigation was handled poorly by local authorities and would likely result in a mistrial.

Portions of the brief are excerpted below:

"Mrs. Streicher is evidently an oversexed woman, high tempered, romantically disposed, and a reader of pulp detective stories. This woman is a born liar who gets satisfaction out of telling lies. She has inherited a domineering disposition from her father, a former German Prussian army officer. She is evidently an outlaw at heart:

rebellious, self-willed, and determined to have her own way at all costs. She is a daydreamer living in a fantasy of outlaw sex life.

"But with all her badness, she loved her son. Every investigator painted (Lucia) much worse than she actually was to bolster their theory that she killed her son. Stories were told of how cruel she was to her son, how she beat him. These stories aroused indignation in the public mind. The stories multiplied and became fixed in the minds of investigators and were accepted by everyone as true. And now what have we? A bad woman, a bad wife, and surely a bad mother, everyone says so and what everyone says must be so... (Mrs. Streicher) must have killed her son because investigators were unable to find anyone else who did the killing."

"In one stroke, the writer of this report undercut months of investigation by the Michigan State Police, the Washtenaw County Sheriff's Department, and the Ypsilanti police. He questions the investigators' working theory and their prime motive— Lucia's freedom from her marriage to be with Clinton LeForge.

"The old triangle comes in handy; that will surely supply the motive (sic). Clinton

LeForge was dragged into this case because of his former relations with Lucia Streicher. It was figured out that the boy was in the way, and if he could be removed, it would leave the road clear for Mrs. Streicher and Clinton LeForge to run away together.

"And if that does not sound good, here's another theory: the boy might have come home and found them in a compromising position, and to shut (the boy's) mouth he (was) killed. Now, this makes everything very simple...But it does not seem to work out that way. It just does not stick.

"When Mrs. Streicher is accused, all the tiger in her disposition is aroused and blazed with fury. She knew she was innocent. Therefore, the fear that assails the guilty was not present with her; the knowledge of her innocence made her strong. All the iron will and egotism inherited from her father came to her rescue.

"Her knowledge that she was right and her accusers were wrong gave her the strength to fight. This aroused (Lucia's) ego, and she made up her mind to put her brains against the brains of the law as represented by the officers investigating the case. She measured their ability by their mistake in accusing her of killing her son. Recalling one of her remarks (after the Leland Hotel surveillance), she said, "I am too damned smart for you. You can't put anything over on me." I think she demonstrated her ability when she made a fool of (Francis Weimar), who tried to entrap her while acting as her friend. As (Lucia's) success in fooling the law mounted, her ego grew, and she became bold and brazen. Her manner and conduct served only to increase the suspicion of the investigators. Lucia was her own worst enemy.

"She (was) an inveterate reader of detective and crime stories and knew all the answers. She was familiar with police methods and delighted in pitting what she felt was her superior intelligence against them, and she won the battle. Not one bit of evidence has been produced against her. There is nothing so far to base a murder charge on.

"And although we heard that Lucia was brutal in her treatment of her son, after close investigation and double checking, we found the stories were hearsay. Lucia was abnormal in almost every way except her mother instinct. In that, she was normal. Deputy Klavitter and I found nothing to contradict this. The mother instinct is not easily thrown aside, AND IN MOST CASES IS NOT."

"What type of man is Clinton LeForge? Little is known about him. He claims to be part or half Indian, but no proof exists for that. He graduated from Detroit College of Law. I am informed that he was always late for class, kept to himself, was an introvert, quite a boxer, and as he himself claims, never forgets a wrong or injury. He was never successful at the practice of law and was an inveterate reader of detective stories. He was known as a "police fan," hanging around the Ypsilanti Police Station all night on many occasions, sitting cross-legged like an Indian.

"This man has come to know all about police methods, as well as the methods of gangsters and crooks. LeForge claims he was instrumental in clearing up the Torch Murders in 1931, but no documentation for that exists. This man is a cheap attorney with a hair-brained imagination. His bad (legal) advice completely upset what little common sense Lucia possessed.

"In my opinion, the accusation against Lucia Streicher can be eliminated. As for her husband, Richard was never under more than a half-hearted suspicion. The only other suspect worth consideration is Clinton LeForge. He has a very good alibi from midafternoon on March 7, 1935, until late at night, except from about six thirty until seven o'clock. By this time, Richie Streicher was already missing. As for the statement made by Martha Dolph that at nine forty-five that night she was walking across the Cross Street Bridge, she heard someone she later identified as Clinton LeForge say, "It's all off now." This overheard remark has no bearing on the killing of Richie Streicher. The boy was already dead at thetime, based on the information from the coroner and also the statement of Mr. and Mrs. Walter Purdy. The Purdys heard a child's screams coming from the footbridge between seven o'clock and seven fifteen. So where are we with this case? One officer who worked the case from the start said to me, "We go around and around and back to where we started and end up nowhere."

It was no wonder Prosecutor Rapp threw up his hands and never brought charges in this case. He was not confident he could get a conviction finding Lucia Streicher or anyone else guilty of this murder. The hearsay testimony of witnesses and the internal disagreement among law enforcement would make a court case futile.

Prosecutor Rapp bowed to public pressure and a request from Governor Franklin Dwight Fitzgerald to call for a one-man grand jury placing all witnesses under oath to get the truth. On September 27, 1937, two years and ten months after Richie's slaying, Washtenaw county circuit Judge George W. Sample opened a one-man grand jury conducted by State Attorney General Raymond W. Starr. In all forty witnesses were called and questioned intensely, but no new evidence was discovered.

Last to be questioned were the Streichers. Judge Sample personally interviewed them for over an hour and stated it was his considered opinion that Mrs. Streicher—in particular—had nothing to do with the murder. Judge Sample also believed Clinton LeForge should be checked out more carefully. In the final analysis, authorities were no closer to making an arrest in the case than they were when the Holt brothers found Richie's body. With no clear motive, murder weapon, witnesses, or confession, no charges were brought in the case. Richie's murder went unavenged, was ultimately relegated to cold-case status, and drifted into obscurity.

Charles Givens, a reporter for the *Detroit Times*, wrote that "In nine out of ten unsolved cases, investigators are virtually certain who the murderer is. Proof is another thing. Ask detectives who handle these cases, and you get the same answer: 'We know who the murderer was, but there were no eyewitnesses or evidence.'" This was one of those cases that eats away at investigators.

—— 11 ——

The Way of All Flesh

Despite decades of enmity, Richard Streicher and Lucia remained married for forty-nine years until her death at the age of sixty-nine on September 20, 1976. She died of a heart attack in their Southfield, Michigan home at seven thirty in the morning. Lucia's remains were cremated on September 23, 1976, at White Chapel Memorial Park in Troy, Michigan—her ashes inurned in the chapel's Shrine of Roses.

Richard survived Lucia by twenty-one years before succumbing to pneumonia on March 28, 1997, at the age of ninety-one. Richard resided at 30051 Marshall Street in Southfield with his surviving spouse, Kathryn Spielburg, and a stepdaughter. Richard's body was cremated at Evergreen Cemetery in Detroit, Michigan.

After the Streicher affair, Clinton LeForge faded from public notice. He was formally disbarred on September 8, 1936. LeForge leased his farmland to run a lumber business and do woodworking. He ran a sawmill powered by a federal truck about one hundred yards behind his farmhouse.

On August 30, 1949, LeForge was rough-sawing timber with a buzz saw when a length of board kicked back, crushing his chest. When LeForge didn't show up for dinner, his wife, Grace, went looking for him. With the buzz saw running unattended, she found her husband on the ground beside the fatal piece of lumber. Washtenaw County Coroner Edwin Ganzhorn pronounced the death an accident. Clinton LeForge is buried at Highland Cemetery in a family plot.

A two-mile stretch of county road north of Eastern Michigan University is named after his farm. That's all that remains of his legacy.

Richard Streicher Jr. was interred in Ypsilanti's Highland Cemetery on Monday, March 11, 1935. Reverend Hugo Fenken of the Emmanuel Lutheran Church conducted the graveside ceremony attended by 150 people. Nobody in living memory can say whether Richie's gravesite ever had a marker. Highland Cemetery has no record a gravestone was ever placed over the unfortunate boy's grave. Perhaps when his body was exhumed, the original grave marker was pushed into the grave when the coffin was reburied. Another theory holds that the parents did not want their son's grave marked because of vandalism fears. Others believe the parents wanted to put their son's murder behind them, and the tombstone would be a reminder to them and the community. Nobody knows. It is difficult to imagine Richie's parents burying him with the indignity of an unmarked grave. Regardless of the reason, Richie's final resting place was left in obscurity for eighty years.

Moved by an article about Richard Streicher Jr., written by John Counts for *The Ann Arbor News* on December 27, 2015, Jackson, Michigan, resident John Sisk Jr. began a GoFundMe page to raise money for a proper gravestone to mark Richie's grave. With the help of Robinson-Bahnmiller Funeral Home in Saline, Michigan; Highland Cemetery in Ypsilanti; and private donations, the site raised $1,500.

A gravestone was purchased and designed to honor Richard Streicher Jr.'s memory. On

Saturday, October 15, 2016, a formal graveside service was presided over by Reverend
Matthew Postiff of Ann Arbor's Fellowship
Bible Church to dedicate the new gravestone. Richie was last seen sledding down
the Four Hills across the street from where
he lived. An image of a sled is engraved in
gray granite with the inscription "Always
Remembered. Never Forgotten." May it be
so.

About the Author

Gregory A. Fournier received his bachelor and master's degrees from Eastern Michigan University and taught English language arts in Michigan and southern California public schools. He has appeared on the Investigation Discovery Channel as a guest expert on serial killer John Norman Collins for their series "A Crime to Remember" in an episode entitled "A New Kind of Monster." More recently, he was interviewed for CBS's "Through the Decades with Bill Kurtis" discussing the Collins murders and his book, *Terror in Ypsilanti*. Greg is also the author of *Zug Island: A Detroit Riot Novel*, and he writes a blog entitled Fornology.com.